THE HOME

Ian Graham

QED

QED Publishing

First published in the UK in 2008 by
QED Publishing
A Quarto Group Company
226 City Road
London EC1V 2TT

www.qed-publishing.co.uk

A catalogue record for this book is available from the British Library.

Printed and bound in China

ISBN 978 1 84538 983 3

Author Ian Graham
Consultant Sue Becklake
Editor Amanda Askew
Designer Gaspard de Beauvais
Picture Researcher Maria Joannou
Illustrator Richard Burgess

Publisher Steve Evans
Creative Director Zeta Davies

Picture credits (t=top, b=bottom, l=left, r=right)
Alamy Images Beaconstox 28t
Apple 21b, 25b
Corbis 22t, The Art Archive/Alfredo Dagli Orti 18t, Bettmann 6b, 20t, 22b, Schenectady Museum/Hall of Electrical History Foundation 4
Courtesy of Brookhaven National Laboratory 26t
Diethelm Keller Brands One Touch 17b
Getty Images AFP Photo/Tsuno 27t, AFP/Toru Yamanaka 11t, David Paul Morris 13t, 23, Ethan Miller 19t, Space Frontiers 9b
Istockphoto 8b, 10–11, 11b, 12–13, 17t
Perific AB 24b
Rex Features 5, 14, 26b
Salton Inc. 15b
Shutterstock 6t, 7t, 8–9, 9t, 16b, 16–17, 18b, 19b, 20b, 21t, 24–25, 25t, 26–27, 28b, 28–29
Sony Computer Entertainment Inc 27b
Topham Picturepoint 15t, ARPL/HIP 10b, Christopher Fitzgerald/ The Image Works 24t, Roger Viollet 16t

Words in **bold** can be found in the glossary on page 30.

Contents

INVENTIONS IN THE HOME

The home is full of inventions. They make your home warm, comfortable and easier to look after, and give you some fun things to do.

Inventing houses

People have not always lived in houses. The house itself had to be invented. The first houses were built about 30,000 years ago. They were made from natural materials, such as stone, wood and even mammoth bones! Then about 9000 years ago, people started building houses made from mud bricks.

Clothes had to be washed by hand until the washing machine was invented in 1851. The first washing machines were operated by hand or by a **steam engine** until the electric washing machine was invented in 1908.

Surprise inventions

Inventions are usually made to solve a problem, but some inventions happen by accident. In 1969, US chemist Spencer Silver was trying to make a strong glue, but his glue turned out to be very weak. In 1974, Arthur Fry used Silver's glue to stick page markers in a book. The weak glue let him peel off the markers and use them again. The result was the Post-it Note.

The digital divide

People in wealthy countries can use the latest inventions in computers, **communications** and the Internet, but people in poorer countries cannot. This is called the digital divide. Some inventors are trying to close the digital divide by producing inventions specially for people in poorer countries. One of these is the wind-up radio. Invented by Trevor Bayliss in 1991, it does not need batteries.

Laptops costing only $100 (£50) have been invented to give children in developing countries the chance to have their own computer.

INVENTIONS IN THE HOME

2000 BCE	Locks
1800 AD	Battery
1850	Dishwasher
1877	Phonograph
1878	Electric light bulb
1905	Portable electric vacuum cleaner
1908	Electric washing machine
1913	Zip fastener
1925	Television
1972	Video cassette recorder
1977	Home computer
1982	Compact Disc (CD)
1996	DVD
1998	MP3 player

SWITCHING ON

The invention of the electric light bulb in the 1800s changed people's lives. Electric lighting let people have light instantly without the danger of gas **flames.**

Electric light

In the early 1800s, people lit their homes with candles, **oil** lamps and gas lights. Fallen candles, spilled oil and leaking gas caused fires. The gas was poisonous, too. Inventors tried to find ways of safely making light. They knew an **electric current** made a thin wire **filament** glow, but the wire quickly burned away. Putting the wire inside a glass bulb and sucking out the air made it work for longer. Without air, the wire would not burn away.

Oil lamps were invented in the Stone Age, when people used shells or hollow rocks to hold the oil.

Thomas Edison's inventions helped to make the light bulb a great success.

Finding a filament

Inventors spent years trying out different materials to make a filament that would glow brightly for a long time. They tried different metals, but found that the chemical, carbon, was the best. In 1878, English chemist Joseph Swan and US inventor Thomas Edison made successful light bulbs.

General Electric Company

Edison's lighting company and a rival company got together in 1892 and formed the General Electric Company. The modern light bulb, with a long-lasting filament made of tungsten metal, was made at General Electric in 1910. Scientists at General Electric also had the idea of filling light bulbs with nitrogen and argon, two gases that would not react with the hot filament, which made light bulbs last longer.

Ordinary light bulbs use a lot of energy. Some countries, including Australia and the UK, now use energy-saving bulbs. These are small **fluorescent lamps** that use less electricity.

Lamps and torches allow people to see, even during the night.

DID YOU KNOW?

The Centennial Light is the longest-lasting light bulb in the world. It was switched on in 1901 and it is still burning today, more than 100 years later! A handmade bulb with a carbon filament, it can be found at Fire Station 6 in Livermore, California, USA.

ZIP UP

People could only use buttons, buckles and pins to do up their clothes until the 1900s, when new fasteners were invented. The zip and Velcro made fastening clothes much easier and quicker.

The zip

Clothes with a lot of buttons or buckles took a long time to do up, so inventors looked for a quicker way. In 1891, US inventor Whitcomb Judson made a shoe fastener with a line of hooks and eyes done up with a slider. It was almost a zip, but not quite. Then in 1913, Swedish engineer Gideon Sunback made a fastener from two lines of metal teeth. Moving a slider one way locked the teeth together. Moving it the other way opened them. He had invented the zip.

Metal teeth

Slider

Pulling a zip's slider opens up the teeth so they can fit between each other or pull apart.

DID YOU KNOW?
Many zips have the letters YKK – Yoshida Company – stamped on them. One factory in Georgia, USA, produces more than seven million zips a day!

Hooks and loops

When Swiss inventor George de Mestral took his dog for a walk one day in 1941, he saw plant seeds covered with tiny hooks stuck in the dog's coat. He wondered if he could make a clothes fastener that worked in the same way. The result was Velcro. It is made of two strips of fabric – one with tiny plastic hooks and the other with tiny loops. When the two strips are pressed together, the hooks catch the loops and they stick together. They can easily be pulled apart and stuck together again.

Each hook and loop in a Velcro fastener forms a very weak link, but hundreds of hooks and loops add together to form a stronger fastening.

The seeds that gave George de Mestral the idea for Velcro were burrs – seeds covered with little hooks.

Astronauts use Velcro to stop things floating around their spacecraft.

Using zips and velcro

Zips are used in all sorts of clothing, including diving suits and flight suits for pilots. They are also used in tents, luggage and backpacks. Velcro fastens thousands of things, from clothes to parts of cars. It is used in spacecraft, too.

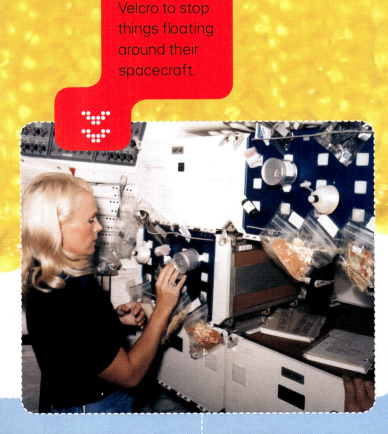

HOME HELP

Homes started to be supplied with electricity in the 1890s. Once homes had electricity, inventors started looking for ways to use it to help with the housework.

Vacuuming up dust

The first vacuum cleaners, invented in the 1860s, were powered by hand. English inventor Hubert Booth built an engine-powered vacuum cleaner in 1901, but it was so big that it had to be parked outside on the road! Chapman and Skinner made an electric vacuum cleaner in 1905, but it was still too big and heavy. Then in 1908, Hoover started selling a smaller, lighter electric vacuum cleaner, invented by James Spangler. By the 1920s, there was a Hoover vacuum cleaner in nearly every US home.

Early vacuum cleaners were as big as a small truck!

Ironing clothes

The electric iron was invented in 1882 by Henry W Seely in New York, USA. Until then, people pressed their clothes with heavy stones or iron blocks heated on a fire. Most irons today are steam irons. The first steam iron went on sale in 1926.

DID YOU KNOW?

In 1978, English inventor James Dyson noticed that vacuum cleaners could not suck up dust very well when their bags became clogged up. Five years and more than 5000 prototypes later, he invented a vacuum cleaner that does not lose suction.

Robot vacuum cleaners went on sale in 2001. They find their own way around a room, sucking up dust as they go.

Doing the washing

The dishwashing machine was invented in the USA in 1850 by Joel Houghton. Turning a handle sprayed water on the dishes, but it did not work very well. US inventor Josephine Cochrane invented the first dishwashing machine that actually worked in 1885. The first electric dishwashers were made in 1913. The electric washing machine for cleaning clothes was invented by Alva Fisher in 1907. He used an electric motor to tumble clothes in a tub full of soapy water.

Dishwashing machines were invented in the 1800s, but they were not popular until they became smaller and cheaper in the 1950s.

TICK TOCK

Thousands of years ago, people used shadows to tell the time. As the Sun moved across the sky, the shadows it made moved, too. But shadow clocks did not work when it was cloudy or at night!

Ancient times

The first clock that did not use the Sun or shadows was the water clock, or a clepsydra. A water clock that is about 3500 years old was found in an Egyptian tomb. Some water clocks worked by dripping water into a jar. Others let water drip out through a hole in the bottom of a jar. The changing depth of water in the jar showed the passing of time.

The sundial is a shadow clock. The Sun casts a shadow on a scale, which shows the time. Shadow clocks were used in ancient Egypt about 5000 years ago.

A clock's pendulum swings and lets the escape wheel turn one tooth at a time.

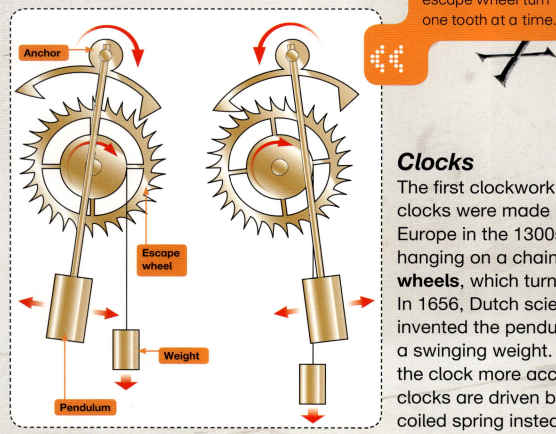

Anchor

Escape wheel

Weight

Pendulum

Clocks

The first clockwork clocks were made in Europe in the 1300s. A weight hanging on a chain turned **gear wheels**, which turned the clock's hands. In 1656, Dutch scientist Christiaan Huygens invented the pendulum clock. A pendulum is a swinging weight. Its swinging action made the clock more accurate. Modern clockwork clocks are driven by the energy stored in a coiled spring instead of a pendulum.

Quartz clocks

Most clocks and watches today are not clockwork, they are electronic quartz clocks. They use pulses of electricity to give them a very accurate electronic 'tick'. Quartz clocks were invented in 1927. Quartz watches went on sale in Japan in 1969.

High-tech watches are now also mobile phones!

DID YOU KNOW?

In 1793, the French tried a different way of dividing up time. The day lasted ten hours instead of 24. Each hour had 100 minutes and each minute had 100 seconds. Clocks and watches were made to show the new time, called decimal time. It only lasted a few years before people went back to the old way of telling the time.

FOOD MATTERS

Since prehistoric times, people have preserved **food by keeping it very cold. At first, food was chilled by snow and ice. By the 1830s, inventors had built machines to chill food. While some scientists worked on chilling food, others worked on new ways of cooking it.**

Keeping cool

The modern refrigerator, or fridge, was the work of several people. One of them was US inventor Jacob Perkins. In 1834, he produced low temperatures by using a liquid called **ether**. As ether **evaporated**, or changed to gas, it took heat out of the food, chilling the food. The ether gas was then squashed to turn it back into liquid and used again. Modern fridges and freezers work in the same way, but with a different liquid.

Some of the latest fridges and freezers are linked to the Internet. You can order groceries, send and receive emails and catch up on the news while you are cooking.

The home fridge

John Gorrie, Alexander Twining and Thaddeus Lowe in the USA, James Harrison in Australia and Carl von Linde in Germany all built refrigeration machines for food and drink businesses in the 1800s. The first fridge made for the home went on sale in 1913 in Chicago, USA.

The first fridges had a big cooling unit on top.

DID YOU KNOW?

The first microwave ovens stood nearly 2 metres in height and weighed about 350 kilograms. They were only used in big businesses where a lot of food had to be cooked quickly. Smaller microwave ovens for the home went on sale in 1967.

Microwaves

During World War II (1939–1945), scientists sent out radio waves, which bounced off the aircraft, telling them where the aircraft was. This is called **radar**. The radio waves were so powerful that they produced heat. One of the scientists, Percy LeBaron Spencer, thought of using short radio waves, called microwaves, to cook food. The oven he made in 1945 was called a microwave oven.

Some microwave ovens read the barcodes printed on food packets. They use the information to set the oven correctly for cooking the food.

Display

Control panel

Barcode scanner

Westinghouse

TIN TOPS

Cans have been used to preserve food for about 200 years. Amazingly, it was nearly 50 years later before anyone thought of inventing a can opener!

Keeping food

In 1795, the French government wanted a way to preserve food for French soldiers. A competition was held and Nicolas Appert won in 1810. He cooked food in glass jars to kill the bugs that would make it rot. Then he sealed the jars shut so that no more bugs could get in. His jars worked well, but they broke easily. In 1810, British inventor Peter Durand solved this problem by using metal cans instead of glass jars.

Nicolas Appert's way of preserving all sorts of food was so successful that it became known as Appertization.

The pop-top or ring-pull can made canned drinks more popular because the cans were tougher than glass bottles and easy to open.

Opening cans

The first can opener was made by US inventor Ezra Warner in 1858. Until then, people had to open cans with a hammer! In the early 1960s, Ermal Fraze from Indiana, USA, invented a new can with a built-in opener. Pulling a metal tab in the top peeled open a slot along lines scored in the metal. In 1965, US inventors Omar Brown and Don Peters replaced the tab with a ring, which was easier to pull. The throw-away rings caused such a bad litter problem that in 1975 Brown and Fraze invented a new ring-pull opener that stayed on the can.

In 1866, J Osterhoudt invented a can that was opened by turning a key to roll the metal lid back.

Electric openers

The electric can opener was invented in Chicago in 1931. A **motor** turned a cutting wheel that moved around the can, cutting through the metal as it went. The first electric can openers had to be plugged into a wall socket. Now, many are powered by battery.

DID YOU KNOW?

About 800 billion cans of all sorts are made every year. Of these, about 220 billion are drinks cans.

Pressing a button starts this battery-powered opener moving around a can to open it.

POCKET POWER

Without batteries, there would be no mobile phones, MP3 players, digital cameras or any other portable electronic gadgets. Batteries are the portable packs of power **that make them work.**

The Leyden jar

Scientists began to understand electricity in the 1740s. A way of storing electricity was invented at the University of Leyden in the Netherlands in 1746, so it was called the Leyden jar. It was a glass jar covered with metal that could be charged up with electricity. In 1800, the Italian scientist Alessandro Volta invented the battery.

Batteries make electricity from **chemical reactions**.

Volta's battery was made from a pile of metal discs – half made of silver and half made of zinc. Pieces of cloth or cardboard soaked in salty water sat between them.

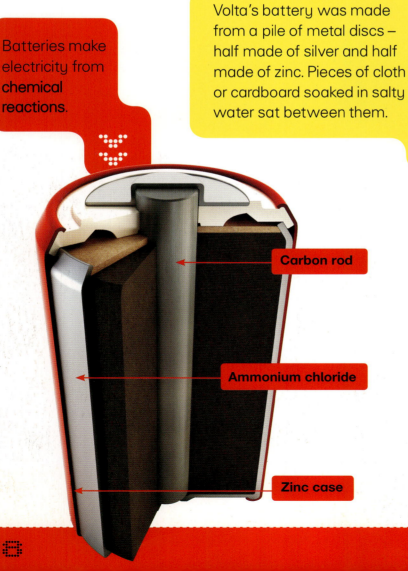

Carbon rod

Ammonium chloride

Zinc case

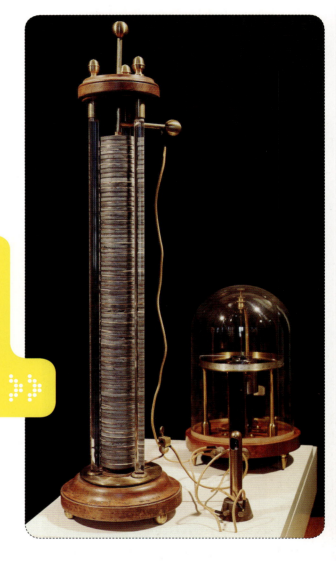

Inside a battery

The first batteries were filled with liquid. It could spill out easily. Today, batteries are filled with a chemical paste instead of liquid and are sealed to stop leaks. They are called dry cells.

Reusable batteries

The energy stored in a battery is used up after a certain amount of time. Most batteries have to be replaced, but rechargeable batteries can be charged up with electricity and used again. The rechargeable battery was invented in 1859 by Frenchman Gaston Planté. The rechargeable batteries in mobile phones and computers today were developed in the 1990s.

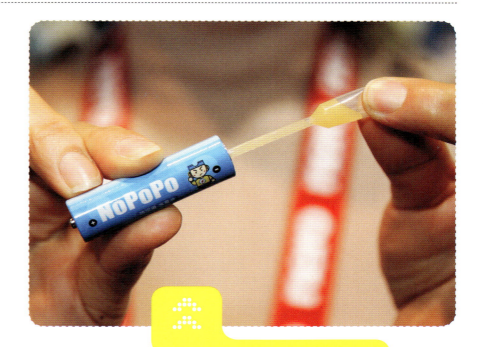

A new type of battery can run on liquids, such as orange juice!

Batteries are recharged in an electrical charger that is plugged into a socket.

DID YOU KNOW?

Born in Italy, Alessandro Volta became a professor of physics. He heard about Luigi Galvani's experiments – where a dead frog's legs twitched when they touched certain metals. Volta carried out some experiments with different metals and ended up making the battery.

MUSIC MACHINES

Today, you can hear music on the radio, television and from music players, including CD players and MP3s. Until the late 1800s, the only way to hear music was to play it yourself or listen to someone else playing it.

The phonograph

The voice of US inventor Thomas Edison saying a nursery rhyme in 1877 was the first sound ever recorded and replayed. Edison had invented a recording machine called the phonograph. Shouting at it made a needle, called a stylus, shake and cut a wiggly groove in a spinning tin cylinder. Ten years later, Emile Berliner invented the gramophone, which recorded sound in the same way on a flat disc.

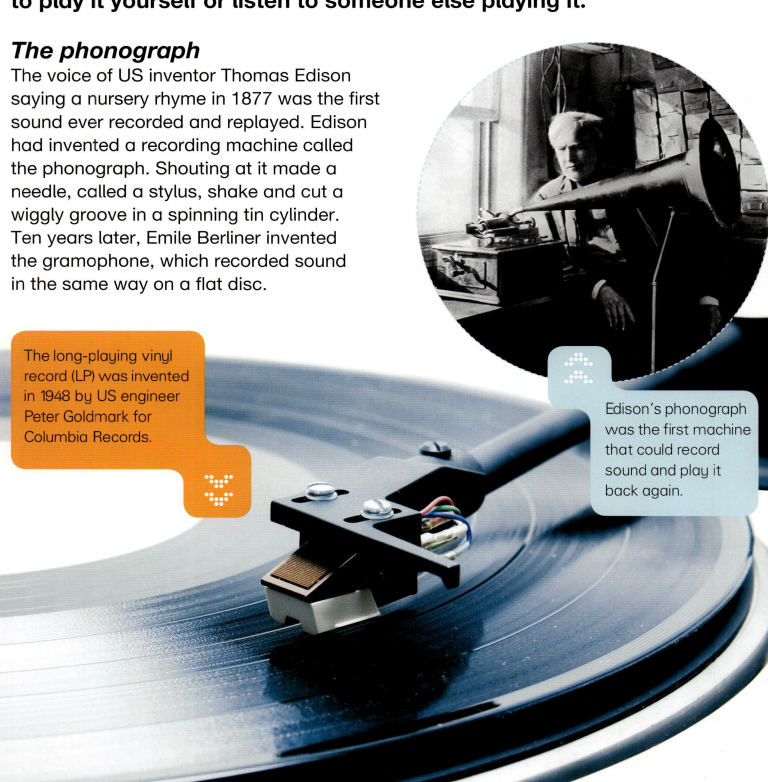

The long-playing vinyl record (LP) was invented in 1948 by US engineer Peter Goldmark for Columbia Records.

Edison's phonograph was the first machine that could record sound and play it back again.

Tapes and CDs

In the 1960s and 1970s, a popular way to listen to recorded music was to use tape cassettes. The plastic tape inside the cassette was covered with magnetic particles. Sound was recorded by **magnetizing** the particles. Dutch engineer Valdemar Poulsen invented magnetic recording in 1898. In 1982, Philips and Sony launched the Compact Disc, or CD. Sound is recorded on a CD as microscopic holes in the silvery disc. The holes are read by shining a **laser** on them.

A tape cassette contained two spools and a reel of magnetic tape.

The iPod was the first music player that could hold 1000 songs. The latest iPods can play video files, too.

MP3

In 1989, the German research institute Fraunhofer-Gesellschaft invented a way of cutting down the amount of information in recorded music so that it could be sent quickly down a telephone line. It was called MP3. The first MP3 players appeared in 1998. Then in 2001, Apple launched its own music player, the iPod.

DID YOU KNOW?

Thomas Edison produced 1093 inventions in telegraphy, telephones, light bulbs, batteries, sound recording and motion pictures – more inventions than anyone else.

ON THE BOX

No one had a television until the 1920s. Now, nearly every home has a television set. Many homes have more than one!

Inventing television

In 1925 in Britain, Scottish electrical engineer John Logie Baird made the first television from wooden boxes, biscuit tins, darning needles and an electric motor. Meanwhile, Isaac Shoenberg in Britain, and Vladimir Zworykin and Philo Farnsworth in the USA built all-electronic televisions. The future of television would be electronic. Baird's television was abandoned.

TV on tape

The first home video recorder was made by Sony in 1964. The first home video cassette recorder was made by Philips in 1972. Video cassettes have now been replaced by DVDs, which were developed by a group of electronics companies in the mid 1990s.

The Video Home System (VHS), created by JVC in 1976, was the most popular home video system for 20 years.

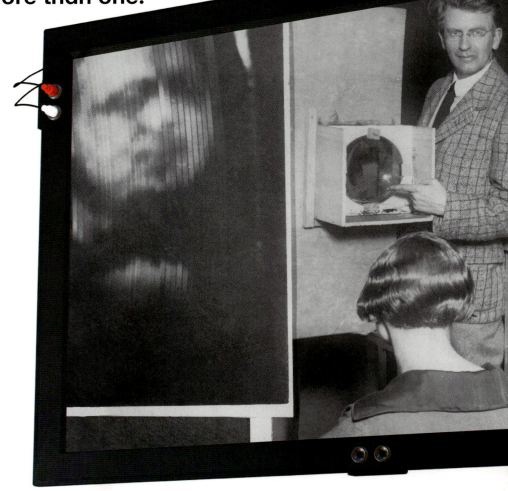

Baird called his television set a televisor. It produced a fuzzy black-and-white picture only 5 centimetres high. A magnifying glass in front of the picture made it look bigger.

DID YOU KNOW?

If you bought a television set in 1930, you would probably have to build it yourself! Most of the Baird television sets were kits that people had to put together. The kits were popular because they were half the cost of a set that was already built.

Skinny screens

For most of television's history, the television screen was the front of a big, heavy glass tube called a cathode ray tube. It was invented in 1897 by Ferdinand Braun. Now there are new thinner, lighter television screens, such as the **plasma** screen. The plasma screen was invented in 1964 by professors Donald Bitzer and Gene Slottow at the University of Illinois, USA.

Panasonic have developed a 3.8-metre plasma screen!

HOME COMPUTERS

The first electronic computers were invented in the 1940s, filling a room with equipment. Since then, computers have become much smaller, lighter and faster.

The Commodore PET computer had a built-in tape recorder for storing programs and data.

Home computers

The home computer was developed in the 1970s. The first three went on sale in 1977. They were the Tandy Radio Shack TRS-80, the Apple II and the Commodore PET. Most home computers at this time had no screen. They were plugged into a television set.

The mouse was invented in 1964 by US inventor Douglas Englebart. The modern Perific mouse is designed to be held and used in different ways.

Making microchips

Two inventions made the home computer possible – the **transistor** and the **microchip**. The transistor was invented in 1947 by US electronics engineers William Shockley, Walter Brattain and John Bardeen. It did the same job as a big glass tube the size of a light bulb, but the transistor was as small as your little fingernail. Then in 1958, another electronics engineer, Jack Kilby, put a group of transistors and other electronic parts together in one small package. He had invented the integrated circuit or microchip.

Shrinking computers

In 1971, US electronics engineer Ted Hoff put all the parts of a computer's master control circuit, the **Central Processing Unit** (CPU), on one chip called a **microprocessor**. The invention of the transistor, the microchip and the microprocessor made the size of computers shrink from the size of a room to the size of a large envelope.

The microprocessor was developed for simple computers, such as the calculator, but is now used in supercomputers.

DID YOU KNOW?

In the early days of computers, people wondered what future computers might be like. In 1949, *Popular Mechanics* magazine looked forward to the day when a computer might weigh less than 1.5 tonnes!

The latest computers are not only more powerful than ever, they are also getting smaller and thinner. The MacBook Air is the thinnest computer notebook in the world.

PLAYING GAMES

The first video games were very simple, but they needed the power of a huge mainframe computer to make them work. Now, video games can be carried in your pocket.

Beginnings

The first video game was created by US physicist Willy Higinbotham at the Brookhaven National Laboratory in Upton, New York, USA, in 1958. It was a bat-and-ball game called Tennis for Two.

Tennis for Two was a video game played on a laboratory instrument called an **oscilloscope**.

Oscilloscope

At first, video games were simple bat-and-ball games, developed by inventors such as Ralph Baer.

Television games

The idea of playing games with a **console** that plugged into your own television set at home was invented by US electronics engineer Ralph Baer in 1951. He created the first video game played on a television set in 1967. It was called Chase. It was another five years before the first home video games console, the Magnavox Odyssey, hit the shops. More than 300,000 of them were bought.

Nintendo Wii is one of the most popular seventh generation video games consoles. Many games are played with a wireless controller, allowing you to physically interact with the game.

DID YOU KNOW?

The leading video games can cost an astonishing £35 million to create. Sales of games consoles and games all over the world are worth more than £15 billion a year.

Generations

New video games consoles are being developed all the time. Each leap in technology produces a new 'generation' of consoles and games. The first video games consoles in the 1970s belonged to the first generation. The latest consoles belong to the seventh generation.

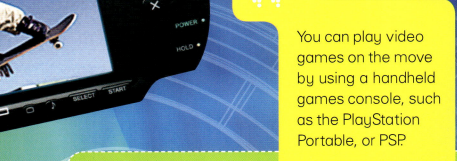

You can play video games on the move by using a handheld games console, such as the PlayStation Portable, or PSP.

ECO-HOMES

More people are trying to lead their lives in ways that are less harmful to the environment. Eco-homes have new types of heating and lighting to save energy.

Electricity from the Sun

One way to make electricity at home is to use energy from the Sun. This is called **solar energy**. It can be changed into other kinds of energy. Solar panels change sunlight into electricity. The panels are made of thousands of small parts called solar cells. The solar cell was invented in 1883 by Charles Fritts. The modern solar cell was invented by Russell Ohl in 1941.

A solar water heater trickles cold water through a pipe in a box called a solar collector. The water absorbs solar energy and heats up.

Heating water

Solar energy can be used to heat water. The modern solar water heater was invented by Clarence Kemp in Baltimore, Maryland, USA, in 1891. Solar water heaters are becoming more popular today as people try to use less electricity and gas at home.

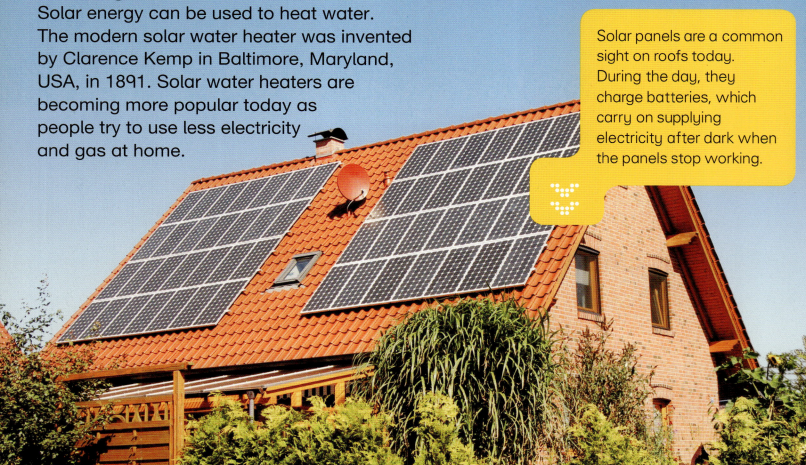

Solar panels are a common sight on roofs today. During the day, they charge batteries, which carry on supplying electricity after dark when the panels stop working.

Wind power

In windy places, a windmill can power a machine that makes electricity. This kind of machine is called a **wind turbine**. The first wind turbine for making electricity was built in 1887 by Professor James Blyth of Anderson's College in Glasgow, Scotland (now Strathclyde University).

DID YOU KNOW?

Wind turbines are a modern kind of windmill. The windmill was invented in about AD 700 in Persia (modern-day Iran) or Afghanistan. The wind pushed around cloth sails, which turned a heavy stone. Grain underneath the stone was ground into flour for making bread.

The biggest wind turbines each produce enough electricity to power up to 5000 homes.

GLOSSARY

Central processing unit (CPU)
The part of a computer that controls the rest of the computer.

Chemical reaction
A process, such as burning, that changes substances by rearranging their atoms.

Communication
Sending information from place to place.

Console
The control box of a video game system.

Electric current
A stream of electricity flowing through something.

Ether
A liquid that evaporates, or changes to gas, very easily.

Evaporate
Change from liquid to gas.

Filament
A thin wire inside a light bulb or electric heater that glows when an electric current flows through it.

Fluorescent lamp
An electric light with a chemical coating that glows when an electric current flows through gas inside the lamp.

Gas
Something that is not solid or liquid, has no shape of its own and expands to fill its container.

Gear wheel
A wheel with teeth around the edge.

Laser
A device that produces an intense beam of pure light.

Magnetize
Make magnetic.

Mainframe
A large computer that is far more powerful than a personal computer, used in industry and operated by specially trained people.

Microchip
An electric circuit built inside a tiny block of plastic.

Microprocessor
A microchip containing all the parts of a computer's central processing unit.

Motor
A machine that uses electricity or another form of energy to make something move or spin.

Oil
A greasy liquid that can be burned to provide light or heat.

Oscilloscope
An instrument used by scientists and engineers to make electrical signals appear as glowing lines on a screen.

Plasma
A gas made of positive and negative electric particles called ions.

Power
The amount of work done every second.

Preserve
Keep something as it is; stop it from changing.

Prototype
The first model of something to be built.

Radar
An electronic system that shows where vehicles, such as ships, aircraft and rockets, are by sending out radio waves and picking up any waves that bounce back from them. Radar stands for radio detection and ranging.

Solar energy
Energy given out by the Sun.

Steam engine
A machine that is powered by steam made by boiling water.

Transistor
A small electronic part used in microchips and other electronic circuits.

Wind turbine
A machine that uses wind to turn a set of long thin blades, which drive a generator to make electricity.

INDEX